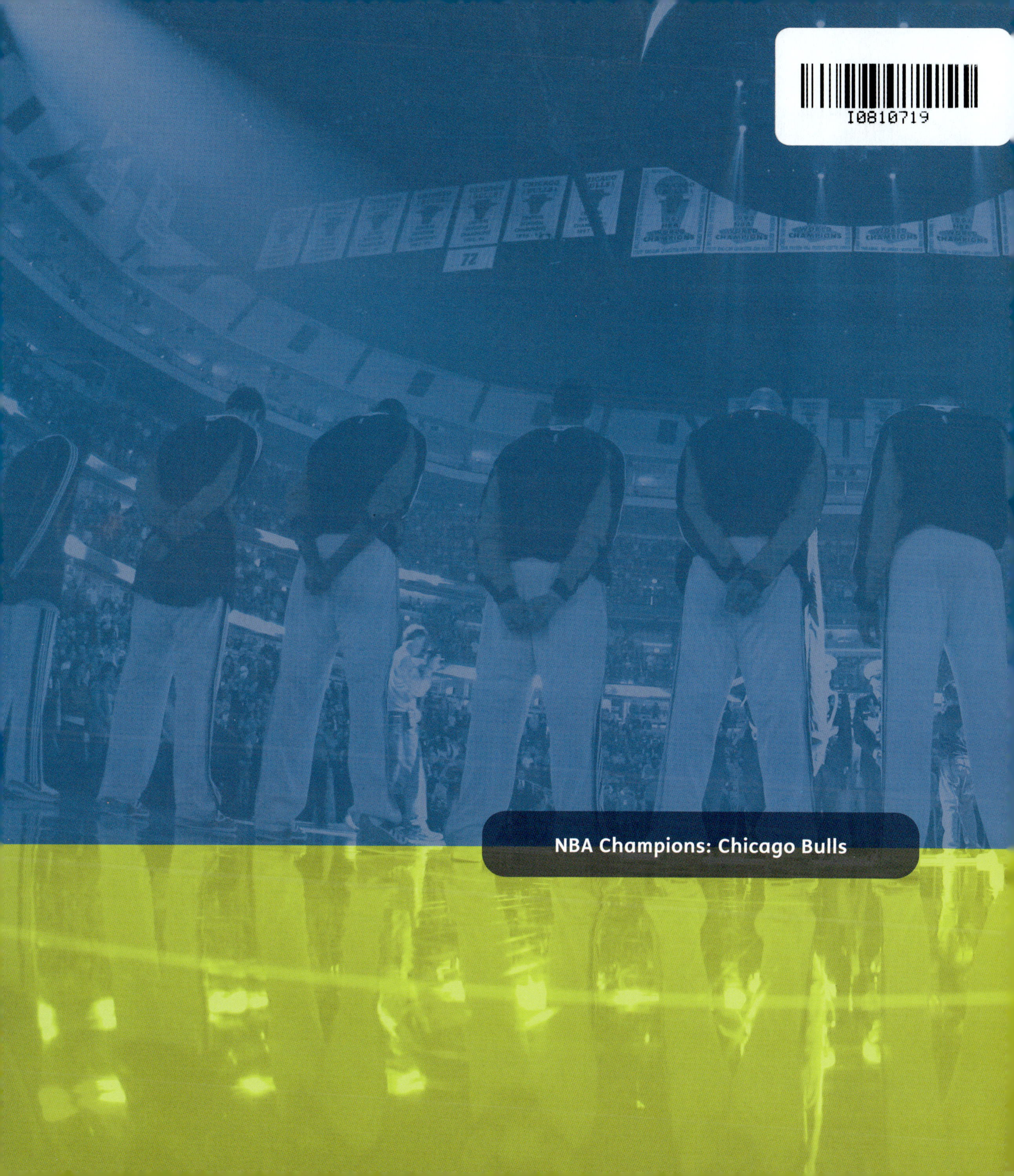

NBA Champions: Chicago Bulls

Small forward Dennis Rodman

NBA CHAMPIONS

CHICAGO BULLS

JOE TISCHLER

CREATIVE EDUCATION / CREATIVE PAPERBACKS

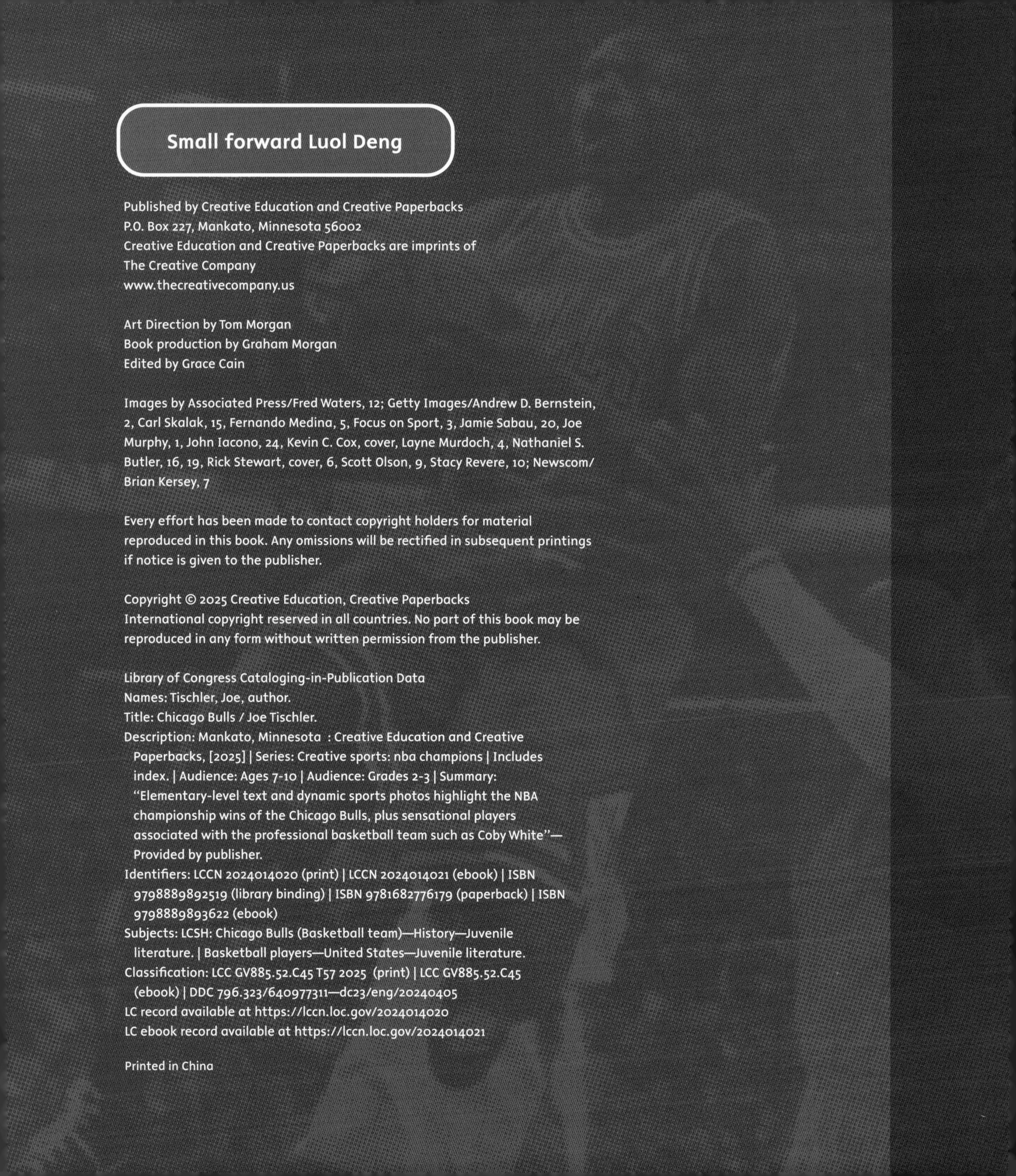

Small forward Luol Deng

Published by Creative Education and Creative Paperbacks
P.O. Box 227, Mankato, Minnesota 56002
Creative Education and Creative Paperbacks are imprints of
The Creative Company
www.thecreativecompany.us

Art Direction by Tom Morgan
Book production by Graham Morgan
Edited by Grace Cain

Images by Associated Press/Fred Waters, 12; Getty Images/Andrew D. Bernstein, 2, Carl Skalak, 15, Fernando Medina, 5, Focus on Sport, 3, Jamie Sabau, 20, Joe Murphy, 1, John Iacono, 24, Kevin C. Cox, cover, Layne Murdoch, 4, Nathaniel S. Butler, 16, 19, Rick Stewart, cover, 6, Scott Olson, 9, Stacy Revere, 10; Newscom/ Brian Kersey, 7

Library of Congress Cataloging-in-Publication Data
Names: Tischler, Joe, author.
Title: Chicago Bulls / Joe Tischler.
Description: Mankato, Minnesota : Creative Education and Creative Paperbacks, [2025] | Series: Creative sports: nba champions | Includes index. | Audience: Ages 7-10 | Audience: Grades 2-3 | Summary: "Elementary-level text and dynamic sports photos highlight the NBA championship wins of the Chicago Bulls, plus sensational players associated with the professional basketball team such as Coby White"— Provided by publisher.
Identifiers: LCCN 2024014020 (print) | LCCN 2024014021 (ebook) | ISBN 9798889892519 (library binding) | ISBN 9781682776179 (paperback) | ISBN 9798889893622 (ebook)
Subjects: LCSH: Chicago Bulls (Basketball team)—History—Juvenile literature. | Basketball players—United States—Juvenile literature.
Classification: LCC GV885.52.C45 T57 2025 (print) | LCC GV885.52.C45 (ebook) | DDC 796.323/640977311—dc23/eng/20240405
LC record available at https://lccn.loc.gov/2024014020
LC ebook record available at https://lccn.loc.gov/2024014021

Printed in China

Point guard Derrick Rose

Shooting guard Michael Jordan

CONTENTS

Home of the Bulls

Chicago, Illinois, is the third largest city in the United States. It sits along the shores of Lake Michigan. It's often called "The Windy City." The city is home to an **arena** called the United Center. It's home to a basketball team called the Bulls.

Forward Jimmy Butler

The Chicago Bulls are a National Basketball Association (NBA) team. They play in the Central Division. That's part of the Eastern Conference. Their **rivals** are the Detroit Pistons and Cleveland Cavaliers. All NBA teams want to win the NBA Finals and become champions. The Bulls have done so six times!

1967 Chicago Bulls

Naming the Bulls

Chicago used to be well-known for its meat packing. The new team owner wanted a name to recognize this. Some of his team name ideas included Toreadors and Matadors. His son said, "That's a bunch of bull." The new team name was born.

Bulls History

The Bulls began play in 1966. They had some early success. They made the playoffs in eight of their first nine seasons. Jerry Sloan and Chet Walker were key leaders. They scored a lot of points. Both are in the Hall of Fame.

The team then fell on hard times. They only made the playoffs twice in nine years. The 1984 NBA Draft changed their history for the good. With the third pick, the Bulls chose Michael Jordan. He became one of the greatest players in NBA history.

Shooting guard Michael Jordan

Forward Toni Kukoč

Jordan was skilled on both ends of the court. He led the league in scoring 10 times. And he was on the NBA All-Defensive Team nine times. He was named NBA **Most Valuable Player (MVP)** five times. That's second most all time.

Phil Jackson became head coach in 1989. He helped build a championship team. Chicago won their first NBA **title** in 1991. They won the championship the next two years, too. It was called a "three-peat." The Bulls performed another three-peat of titles from 1996–98.

Other Bulls Stars

Scottie Pippen was one of Jordan's most important teammates. He was on all six Bulls' title teams. He was an **all-star** seven times. Dennis Rodman could get a lot of **rebounds**. So could Horace Grant.

Small forward Scottie Pippen

Shooting guard Zach LaVine

Derrick Rose was a great point guard. He scored a lot of points and gave a lot of **assists**. He won an NBA MVP award. Rose was teammates with Jimmy Butler and Joakim Noah. They helped the Bulls win a lot of games.

Zach LaVine and DeMar DeRozan lead the Bulls today. Bulls fans hope they can help bring another championship to Chicago soon!

NBA CHAMPIONS

About the Bulls

First season: 1966–67

Conference/division: Eastern Conference, Central Division

Team colors: red and black

Home arena: United Center

NBA CHAMPIONSHIPS:

1991, 4 games to 1 over Los Angeles Lakers

1992, 4 games to 2 over Portland Trail Blazers

1993, 4 games to 2 over Phoenix Suns

1996, 4 games to 2 over Seattle SuperSonics

1997, 4 games to 2 over Utah Jazz

1998, 4 games to 2 over Utah Jazz

TEAM WEBSITE:

https://www.nba.com/bulls/

Glossary

all-star—a player picked to play in the All-Star Game, featuring the season's top stars

arena—a large building with seats for spectators, where sport games and entertainment events are held

assist—a basketball pass that leads to a basket

Most Valuable Player (MVP)—an honor given to the season's best player

rebound—getting the ball after a missed shot

rival—a team that plays extra hard against another team

title—another word for championship

Shooting guard Jerry Sloan

Index